GW00492822

Rest
Replenish
Restore

ESSENTIAL SELF-CARE
TIPS AND REMEDIES

LINDA GRAY

summersdale

REST, REPLENISH, RESTORE

An Hachette UK Company
www.hachette.co.uk

Summersdale Publishers Ltd
Part of Octopus Publishing Group Limited
Carmelite House
50 Victoria Embankment
LONDON
EC4Y 0DZ
UK

www.summersdale.com

Printed and bound in Malta

ISBN: 978-1-78685-804-7

Substantial discounts on bulk quantities of Summersdale books are available to corporations, professional associations and other organisations. For details contact general enquiries: telephone: +44 (0) 1243 771107 or email: enquiries@summersdale.com.

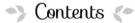 Contents

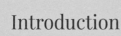

Introduction

If you are feeling tired, careworn or troubled, *Rest, Replenish, Restore* can ease your mind. Packed with tips, affirmations and ideas, this book will help soothe you and bring balance back to your emotional and spiritual life. There are also recipes for remedies to invigorate you and give you a mental and physical pick-me-up.

Each suggestion can be personalised to suit your lifestyle and tailored to best tackle your own needs. Keep this book handy and experiment with the ideas, recipes and affirmations to create a healing routine that works best for you. Treat yourself to the beautifully balanced mind, body and spirit that you deserve.

MIND

Science has identified many functions of the brain and yet, despite extensive research, our minds still hold mysteries that to date continue to elude us. We do know that our minds can often surprise us! We all experience random thoughts, that can deeply affect our mood. This chapter examines proactive ways to focus our mind into thinking more positively, and demonstrates ways to dispel negative thought processes.

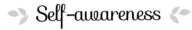 Self-awareness

Self-awareness is a powerful tool but will require a little practice before you become really good at it. The secret is to observe what you are thinking at the present moment. Don't make it a chore – we can't possibly observe and identify every thought we have – but a little awareness every so often can really help! This moment could be while you are at work, washing dishes, exercising, or at any other point during the day. Simply observe your present moment thought. What are you thinking about right now?

Once you have identified the thought, decide if it serves you or not. If it doesn't, bring your focus back to the present moment. For example, if you are reading a book at bedtime and find yourself thinking about work, bring yourself back to the story you are reading. You'll sleep much better if you enjoy the present moment!

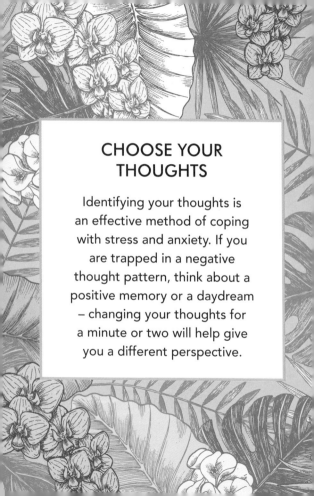

CHOOSE YOUR THOUGHTS

Identifying your thoughts is an effective method of coping with stress and anxiety. If you are trapped in a negative thought pattern, think about a positive memory or a daydream – changing your thoughts for a minute or two will help give you a different perspective.

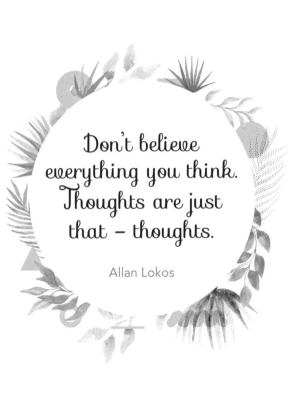

Don't believe
everything you think.
Thoughts are just
that — thoughts.

Allan Lokos

IGNORE NEGATIVE THOUGHTS

Think beyond your present worrisome thought and remember there is always a solution, even when your brain might be telling you the opposite. You have the power to break free of your negative train of thought.

MASTERING
YOUR THOUGHTS

When you have identified your thought, and decided if it serves you, play a little game with your brain and find an opposing thought that makes you feel a lot better. Maybe you are feeling overwhelmed and thinking 'How am I going to get the house cleaned?' Replace that thought with an alternative, such as 'Getting physical will make me feel good, and the house will look wonderful when I've finished.' Then load your favourite playlist and get going!

In this moment
I am free of worry
and at peace.

Understanding those Thoughts

Humans have a crazy number of thoughts every day and many of them are on repeat. Give yourself permission to put the past to rest and come up with some new thoughts instead. Many thoughts we have can come from the collective consciousness – this means that we absorb ideas from the media, a little local gossip or an advertisement online. As a result we find ourselves dwelling on an issue that may have very little to do with our own lives. If you find yourself drifting down this path, stop and ask yourself whether this thought is actually serving you and whether or not it is relevant to your own life, or the lives of your family or friends. As soon as you have answered the question, you can explore the idea or let it go.

Tragedies occur and if there is nothing you can do about it at this red hot minute, try to focus on a positive news item. There are lots of good things happening in the world to counter the negative.

Find the Good News

Actively seek out the good news items. They do exist. Kind, wonderful people are doing some great things out there. Home in on that and allow the bad news to take a back seat. Appreciating kindness and positive energy will steer your thoughts away from worry and towards constructive solutions.

All our dreams
can come true if we
have the courage to
pursue them.

Walt Disney

I ACTIVELY SEEK OUT GOOD NEWS EVERY DAY.

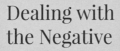

Dealing with the Negative

Life is a challenge but consuming a lot of news, watching or reading dark and 'edgy' content or reading magazines that encourage idealised bodies and shame others can also have a negative effect on you.

Keep a mood diary handy; a simple exercise book will do. Then make a note of how you are feeling throughout each day. Identify the activities linked to your lesser moods. This will empower you and help to avoid those downward mood swings in the future.

DEALING WITH THE MEDIA

Don't forget that you have a choice. You don't have to check social media every 5 minutes! Allow yourself some digital detox time. Leave your phone in another room at night and use an alarm clock instead of your phone. Go for a leisurely walk without devices so that you can simply appreciate your environment and reconnect with nature, free from all distractions.

Anxiety

Anxiety is a result of thinking about what may or may not happen in the future. Anxious feelings surface when we project negative thoughts and memories from the past onto our future. We can combat anxiety by realising that the past is gone and that we can choose to see a different future – one that we can create for ourselves.

The ability to choose to foresee a different, positive future is a powerful one. When you are feeling anxious, close your eyes for a moment and visualise an alternative outcome. This action can reduce anxiety. Accept and be happy that you are the creator of your own reality and choose to live the life you desire instantly.

PROMISE YOURSELF

Make time during the day to daydream. A few moments spent imagining your ideal life while washing dishes or while you are in the shower will help reduce anxiety, give you a respite from worry and allow solutions to surface.

Don't Worry

Remember that worrying never achieved anything. A Shantideva quote sums it up perfectly: 'Why worry if you can do something about it; and why worry if you cannot do anything about it?' When you find yourself losing sleep over something, write down what it is you are worrying about. Then repeat the Shantideva quote to yourself and decide – whether you are able to take action or not – that you will let go of your worry.

Remedy for headaches

To ease headaches try making your own soothing mint balm. The naturally fresh and cooling scent of the herb is ideal for this remedy. Once prepared, the balm can be stored in a small jar or tin for up to 6 months. You can carry it with you when you are on the go or keep it stashed at the ready in your home. A few dabs gently massaged into your temples can be very effective.

INGREDIENTS:

200 ml sunflower oil
2 tbsp dried mint leaves (crushed)
20–30 drops of peppermint oil
50 g beeswax

METHOD:

Place the oil and mint leaves in a heavy-based pan and simmer on a low heat for approximately one hour so the herbs infuse the oil. Remove from heat, cool and strain, retaining the oil. Add the peppermint oil drops to the infused sunflower oil.

Place the beeswax in a bowl and melt over a bain-marie. Once the wax has melted stir in the infused oil, then pour the mixture into a clean glass jar or lidded tin.

FEEL THE JOY

Visualise yourself succeeding at whatever it is you want to achieve, be it passing an exam or paying the mortgage this month. Anticipate the success and joy you will feel when you achieve your goals.

❧ Stress ❧

Stress is part of the human condition. A low level of stress for a short period of time is normal and won't impact your health. Continued stress can and will eventually affect your well-being and can cause many unwelcome physical conditions, ranging from headaches and migraines to muscular pain and stiffness and, in extreme cases, heart problems. Worrying about future results, whether it's taking your driving test, starting your own business, or any other goal, will often cause a level of stress that negatively impacts you both physically and mentally.

The best way to deal with this level of stress is to remember that failure is just a way to learn and improve on whatever it is you are striving for. Then give it your best shot.

SUCCESS
is the ability
to go from failure
to failure without
losing your
ENTHUSIASM.

Winston Churchill

JUDGEMENT

Oh, how we like to judge! However compassionate we sometimes feel towards our fellow man, it is so easy to judge. For example, when someone is brisk with us we instantly think 'how rude', making a judgement about that person. In fact, we do it to ourselves all the time! Negative self-judgement generates feelings that we are not good enough. 'I'm not worthy' is one of the most common feelings underlying many issues we have, from substance addiction to anxiety.

Practise loving yourself. Appreciate your whole self, including those body parts you normally judge negatively, and remember you are unique. There never has been and never will be another 'You'!

YOU ARE UNIQUE

Love yourself. Ignore your self-doubting and judgemental thoughts and remember everyone is unique in their own special way. Make a success journal. List every success you've had, however small, and continue to record daily successes in your journal – even getting the kids to go to bed at a reasonable time is a success! Be happy in your own uniqueness. You are special.

I AM A UNIQUE, WORTHY HUMAN BEING AND SPREAD LOVE AND HAPPINESS TO EVERYONE I MEET.

Smile

A smile goes a long way.
Smiling at someone when you
are out and about could make
their day and will definitely
make you feel better!

Laughter

One of the best ways to improve your mood is to laugh. Laughter releases all sorts of feel-good stuff and gives you a chance to let go of any negative thoughts that have been playing on your mind. Choose a funny video online or watch an episode of your favourite sitcom.

It has been scientifically proven that laughter and happy thoughts can even cure physical illness so a little chuckle here and there will certainly alleviate worrisome thoughts. If you can't find time right now to watch a video, remember the last time you laughed out loud and then smile to yourself as you relive the moment.

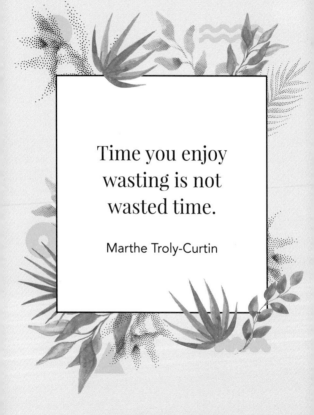

Time you enjoy
wasting is not
wasted time.

Marthe Troly-Curtin

Positive Images

We use our five senses to interpret images, sounds, tastes, smells and the feeling of solid objects. Use your sense of sight to trigger happy thoughts. Seek out pictures that bring back happy memories, like a photo of a fabulous holiday you had or a beautiful island you'd like to visit one day.

If you're struggling for inspirational images from your own life, perhaps put up a picture of a cute animal. Studies show that humans feel all sorts of positive emotions when they see a baby animal such as a puppy or a kitten. It's simple – but it works!

PIN-UPS

Think of some words that inspire positive feelings, such as love, courage, trust, kindness and compassion. Write these on coloured paper or card – the better to catch your eye – and pin them up next to the bathroom mirror or over the sink. Make a point of contemplating the meaning of those words every time you see them.

I WILL
APPRECIATE
THE BEAUTY
IN MY WORLD
TODAY.

Remedy for a low immune system

Turmeric is so brightly coloured that one assumes that it contains some sort of pick-me-up properties. Well, it does: the antioxidant, antibacterial, antiviral and anti-inflammatory properties of the plant can improve the body's immune function. Turmeric tea is perhaps one of the most effective ways of consuming the spice. So, make time in your day to sit down and relax with a cuppa – not only will it be good for your soul but it will also be good for your body.

INGREDIENTS:

1 tbsp fresh or dried turmeric root, grated*
1 cup of hot boiled water

METHOD:

Place the grated turmeric in a loose leaf tea infuser and steep in hot water. The longer you leave it, the more infused it will be – try drinking after 5 minutes of steeping initially. You can prepare large quantities, allowing the tea to brew for a longer period. Store this in a fridge and simply reheat the required amount in a pan.

*If you cannot source turmeric root, the powdered variety can be used as a substitute, although it is best to strain this prior to drinking to avoid a gritty texture.

NATURE'S MUSIC

Experiment with sounds. Listen to birds singing in the garden or whale music. These sounds will make you feel joyful and closer to nature. Be alert to the natural sounds that surround you as you walk in the forest or the garden.

SING AND DANCE

Make a point of listening to your favourite music. Even 5 minutes of beautiful music or your favourite dance track will boost your mood and may even get you singing along. Sing while you're washing up or hoovering. You might attract a few odd looks but your positivity will become infectious. A home full of singing people is a happy place.

If you listen to a dance track you can move and dance to the rhythm thereby releasing lots of feel-good hormones and changing your mood instantly.

Whether you
think you can or
you think you can't,
you're right.

Henry Ford

SMELL THE ROSES

Many people find that certain scents evoke strong memories. Find a scent that evokes a memory of a happy moment. It could be anything from the smell of a favourite soup Granny used to make to the smell of lavender on a warm summer's day. Reminding yourself of a happy memory will bring peace to the present moment.

If you can't recall a particular scent, create scent memories for yourself. Make a point of smelling things. Smell your food before you eat; smell the flowers in the garden or your local park. You'll be engaging with your world in a new and mindful way – and you'll be smelling pleasant odours all day!

Herbs

Plant a few sweet-smelling herbs
in pots and place them on a well-lit
windowsill. Grow basil or coriander
or even a small lavender plant. Rub
the leaves from time to time and enjoy
the natural scents – and you can add
chopped herbs to your meals as well.

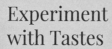

Experiment with Tastes

Try something new! There is a huge choice of herbs, spices and varieties of fruit and veg available to experiment with. There's nothing wrong with an occasional old favourite, but trying out different ideas for new recipes can encourage you to develop your palate and discover new flavours. It's surprising how good you feel when you eat healthy food – not only for the physical benefits but your mind will also profit from your healthy eating habits!

And when you do give in to that occasional treat don't feel guilty, just savour the moment.

SAVOUR THE TASTES

Take your time when you eat.
Enjoy the taste of each mouthful,
chew it well and savour the
moment of feeding your body
nutritious food. Your digestive
system will thank you for
slowing down a little as well.

It's not what
happens to me,
but how I react to
it that matters.

Remedy for feeling stressed

What is more relaxing than resting your feet in a warm footbath to soak away the stress of the day? The addition of some naturally calming herbs simply enhances this experience. Why not make it a daily bedtime ritual?

INGREDIENTS:

Any, or a mixture, of the following dried herbs:
Chamomile
Lemon balm
Lavender
Rose petals
Warm water (approximately 100 g herbs to every 2 litres of water)

METHOD:

Place water and herbs in a pan and bring to the boil. Simmer for 30 minutes. Remove from heat to allow herbs to steep for a further hour, then strain. Reheat the water before use and add to a basin large enough to wiggle your feet in (a washing-up bowl would take approximately 4 litres of water and 200 g herbs). Soak for as long as desired but try not to fall asleep!

Touch and Feel

Stop for a moment and engage with the textures and surfaces around you. If your hands feel hot, smooth your hands over a hard, cool surface in the kitchen or elsewhere in your home. If you feel cold, warm yourself with your favourite throw or blanket. Hold it close and be mindful of the feel of the material against your skin.

TEXTURES

Enjoy nature's textures. Feel the grass beneath your bare feet or the softness of a flower petal between your fingertips. Connecting with nature through your senses will always make you feel good and in awe of the world around you.

Change your
thoughts and you
change your world.

Norman Vincent Peale

Breathe

Find stillness in the moment by practising mindful breathing. Simply focus on the act of breathing in and out; it will give you a moment's respite from thinking about whatever is on your mind.

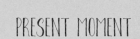

PRESENT MOMENT

Accept the present moment for what it is. If your mind is battling with a problem, the more you think about it, the less you allow a solution to suggest itself.

Consciously shift your thoughts to a pleasing scenario for a moment or two and allow yourself to envision the successful outcome of your project. The next moment could offer an idea that could change your life, or at the very least suggest a solution to your problem.

THIS TOO
SHALL PASS.

Brain Dump

Feeling overwhelmed is a common malady in today's fast-paced lifestyle. It can keep you stuck in the state of stress and anxiety. Tackle this by allotting 30 minutes to work through the jobs that have been bothering you. Write your most pressing problem in the centre of a sheet of paper and then around it scribble down all the issues you have with the problem. For example, 'How do I keep up with the housework?'

Then write the details that are bothering you, such as 'mess piles up in the kitchen' or 'I never have enough clean sheets'. Getting into the nitty gritty of a problem can force a solution to jump out at you. It may be simply 'I'll wash up while I cook' or 'I'll always wash two sets of sheets at the same time'. The overwhelming feeling of having too much on your plate will be reduced by writing down your issues and finding solutions.

MAKE A LIST

Too much to do? Make a list or two. Invest in a couple of pads and a decent pen rather than using your phone or laptop. A written to-do list gives you the satisfaction of crossing off tasks as you complete them.

Remedy for poor mental focus

Rosemary is a herb that has been used in traditional medicine to improve memory power. It has naturally occurring properties that inhibit nerve cell damage. Fresh smelling and fragrant, a simple rosemary infusion can help sharpen your mental focus.

INGREDIENTS:

2 tsp of dried or fresh rosemary
500 ml water
1 tsp honey (optional)

METHOD:

Place the water and rosemary in a pan and bring to the boil. Simmer for 5–10 minutes to allow the flavour of the herb to infuse the water. Strain and retain the fluid, then sit back to enjoy your infusion immediately. A teaspoon of honey can be added if desired to soften what can otherwise be a slightly sharp flavour. This infusion should not be used during pregnancy and is not recommended for those with anticoagulation problems.

BODY

Poor body image is possibly one of the most common causes of stress in the Western world today. External influences and constant reminders of what is and isn't 'good' for us can cloud our vision to the point of not knowing what to do for the best. This chapter is designed to help you remind yourself what a beautiful and wonderful entity your body is. Take a few ideas from the following pages and turn them into a daily practice so that you can enjoy your wonderful body.

Nutrients

If you have been feeling sluggish for a while, tune in to your magnificent body and make sure you are nourishing it on a daily basis. The five-a-day mantra is a good place to start but you can also top up your nutrition by replacing your supermarket fruit and veg with organic, fresh, locally sourced produce.

The best way to get the nutrients you need is to up your portions. You could graze all day on fruit and veg, as long as you have variety. For example, avocados are high in (good) fats and calories and many fruits contain a high fructose content. Mix it up and enjoy new tastes.

SALADS

Simple salad leaves could be
available practically all year
round from your own windowsill
or backyard. Experiment with
hanging baskets full of 'cut and
come again' varieties of lettuce
and remember to use them!

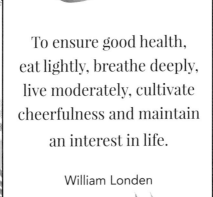

To ensure good health,
eat lightly, breathe deeply,
live moderately, cultivate
cheerfulness and maintain
an interest in life.

William Londen

Buy Organic

Seek out delivery services of fresh produce from local farms, or visit them if you can because their fruit and veg are usually fresher than supermarket produce. Alternatively, shop at a greengrocer or market. In any event, try to buy organic to avoid consuming chemicals or insecticides.

Diet Slowly

Have you been holding on to a few extra pounds? Following one diet after another is often counter-productive. Diets that promise fast weight loss are appealing but when you hit the first plateau of weight loss it's easy to get discouraged. You're also likely to put the lost pounds back on again.

Be realistic. It's taken you a while to put on those pounds; it's going to take a while to lose them. Aim to lose a pound a week. This may seem like a long, slow business, but doing it slowly gives your body a chance to adjust to its new weight and you're less likely to pile on the pounds later.

I LOVE MY
BODY JUST THE
WAY IT IS AND
I AM TREATING
IT WELL
EVERY DAY.

WHAT TO EAT

There are many fad diets, and hundreds of 'scientific' posts on social media and in the news informing us of the latest food scare. Some of them may be entirely justified but we aren't all in a position to buy high-priced super-foods. Read too many theories and you'll end up not knowing what on earth is safe to eat!

We are all very different, and the most important diet to keep to is one that suits you personally, taking into consideration nutrition and any health needs that you may have. A good general guideline when buying ready-made food is to check on the packaging for the ingredients and choose products that have a lower sugar content.

TUNE IN

Listen to your body. Decide what
works best for you by tuning
in to your body's reactions
to certain foods. If you feel
sluggish in the morning, consider
the foods you ate yesterday
and adjust your diet today.

The more you eat,
the less flavour; the
less you eat, the
more flavour.

Chinese proverb

CALORIE COUNTING

Consult with your doctor before cutting calories or restricting your food intake. Keeping your calories around your recommended daily allowance will help your mood and energy levels to remain stable.

LIFESTYLE CHOICES

If you have an office-based job you might feel that you're mired at your desk all day and struggle to get enough exercise. Stop and consider your lifestyle and if you feel you really are sitting around too much every day, promise yourself to get a little extra exercise.

You don't have to join an expensive gym and work out like crazy every day. Simply take a walk – preferably in nature. If that's not possible, treat yourself to a 15- or 20-minute walking workout. There are plenty of videos on YouTube. Choose one you resonate with and commit to it every day.

I AM MOVING
MY BODY EVERY
DAY AS IT WAS
DESIGNED
TO MOVE.

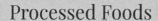

Processed Foods

Don't be tempted by low-fat fast-food products as they are often packed with extra sugar and salt. Our bodies actually digest and expel fats a lot easier than sugar. Don't get caught by 'sneaky' sugars disguised as health food – check the food packaging to see whether the low-fat item is packed with sugars and salts.

Sticking to natural products as much as possible will result in a healthy body and, as organic products are becoming more widely available, more money in your pocket! With social media exposing non-foods – highly processed food that require added artificial vitamins – many supermarkets are beginning to stock organic and healthier foods. Seek them out and your body will thank you.

Supporting
Healthy Options

Make a point of asking your local supermarket or high street shops if they sell organic and healthier alternatives to products you are looking for – and if they do, purchase them. Supermarkets react positively to customer feedback and even more so to customers' money! The more organic and healthy products that are bought, the more they'll stock.

GROW YOUR OWN

Have you any outside space?
Many fruits and vegetables can
be grown in containers and large
pots, such as beetroot, broad
beans, carrots, French beans,
herbs, peas, potatoes, radishes,
rocket, tomatoes, chillies, peppers,
salad leaves and spring onions.
Having fresh organic food at
your fingertips is achievable
and not difficult to maintain.

Ratatouille

A great vegetarian recipe that you can adjust according to the contents in your fridge or garden.

INGREDIENTS:

1 or 2 courgettes
1 aubergine
1 or 2 onions
1 tin of tomatoes – or use fresh ripe tomatoes
   if available

METHOD:

Slice courgette(s) and prepare aubergine by slicing or cutting into chunks.

Sometimes aubergines can be slightly bitter. To avoid this, cut in half and lay cut sides down in a little salt for about an hour. This draws out any bitter juices. Rinse well.

Peel and cut onion(s) into small pieces.

Put all the prepared vegetables into a large pan with chopped tomatoes – tinned or fresh.

Cook over a low–medium heat until vegetables are cooked through.

Stir in chopped fresh herbs if available and if desired. Basil works well as it brings out the tomato taste, but any preferred herbs will work. Season with a little salt and pepper but taste first in case you don't need to season.

Serve as a side dish or on toast as a delicious lunchtime snack.

Tip: This recipe can often taste even better on day two. Make twice as much as you need. Leave leftovers to cool completely, store in the fridge overnight and then simply reheat the next day.

COLOURISE YOUR DIET

Red fruits and vegetables are high in antioxidants which help eliminate free radical cells from our bodies. The redder the better. Add a few raspberries or strawberries to your breakfast cereal or morning smoothie. Or try slicing a few strawberries into a green salad. Beetroot is an excellent source of folic acid and potassium and can be added to smoothies or salads.

Hobbies

Are you so tired at the end of the working day that you find yourself slumped in front of the TV? Resting is good but sometimes our energy levels can also be replenished through fresh mental stimulation.

If you absolutely have to have the TV on, take up a hobby that you can enjoy alongside it. Try a needlecraft or use your artistic skills to create greetings cards for family and friends. Many hobbies can be inexpensive and very satisfying. You may even end up developing a cottage industry – it happens!

Bedtime

Check in with yourself to see whether your bedtime routine is a ritual that is serving you well. Sleep is so important, and lying in bed with millions of thoughts and worries plaguing your mind will not result in a deep and relaxing sleep. Develop a mindset that sets you up for a good night's sleep.

If taking a bath relaxes you, schedule in the time to enjoy a bath before bedtime. Switch off your electronic devices and dim the lights. One of the most effective ways to clear your mind is to make a list. In the evening write down what you want to achieve the next day.

The list could include finishing a big work project or simply putting out the recycling boxes. Big or small, capturing the tasks on paper will stop them rushing around in your mind as you drift off to sleep because your mind knows you don't have to remember them; they are all written down!

In the end, it's not
the years in your life
that count. It's the
life in your years.

Abraham Lincoln

TURN OFF THE LATE NEWS

If you're an avid consumer of current affairs and have trouble sleeping, try switching the channel or closing the website at least an hour before you go to bed. This will give you time to decompress from all the new information you've been consuming.

When I get into bed,
I relax and sleep deeply,
waking refreshed
and energised in
the morning.

Declutter

Get a good night's sleep: declutter your bedroom, remove work-related items, leave your phone downstairs if possible and drop all dirty laundry in the basket before you get into bed. Decluttering helps to create a calm environment, which is exactly what you need at bedtime!

Tisanes

The plants that grow on our beautiful planet are abundant with healing properties. Do a little research and you will be astounded by what we can heal without resorting to pharmaceutical drugs. Of course there is a place for conventional medicines, especially those prescribed by your doctor, but sometimes a little natural healing will soothe you.

If you are having trouble sleeping, even after you've improved your bedtime routine, find a natural remedy to calm you before bed. Tisanes are simply herbs infused in hot water. Lemon Balm Tea is soothing and easy to make, especially if you have a lemon balm plant growing in your garden. Pick a sprig or two, pour on freshly boiled water and leave to infuse for about 5 minutes. Then enjoy the soothing taste to help relax you before bedtime.

It is HEALTH
that is
REAL WEALTH
and not pieces
of gold and silver.

Mahatma Gandhi

Exercise

Choose to be healthy today. Before you leap into the first aerobic workout or complicated yoga session, honestly assess your fitness. It's easy to think we are fitter than we are, especially if we are rushing around all day at work or with kids, or both.

Check out some videos online that appeal to you and try a few to see what level of difficulty is right for you. Take your age and your lifestyle into consideration when selecting a workout and, most importantly, choose something you'll enjoy. It could be a dance session, a weight-based programme or any number of other ideas to get your body moving. Once you've found a suitable workout timetable/plan, stick with it until it's finished; you'll feel a wonderful sense of achievement when you succeed in completing the workout.

HEALTHY RESEARCH

Learning will encourage you to develop and improve your health. Research healthy lifestyle tips and apply them to your own life.

I AM
ENERGISING
MY BODY WITH
EXERCISE
EVERY DAY.

Remedy for insomnia

Having trouble sleeping? Try this soothing drink; it couldn't be easier to prepare. Milk helps boost the sleep-inducing hormone melatonin, and combining it with cinnamon, a spice that has antifungal, antibacterial and antiviral properties, can be a fabulous tonic. Prepare just before bedtime to help you relax into a restful sleep.

INGREDIENTS:

1 cup of milk
¼ tsp cinnamon powder
2–3 drops vanilla essence
1 tsp agave syrup or honey

METHOD:

Place the milk, cinnamon and vanilla essence in a pan and gently simmer. Remove from the heat before it boils. Add the agave syrup or honey to taste.

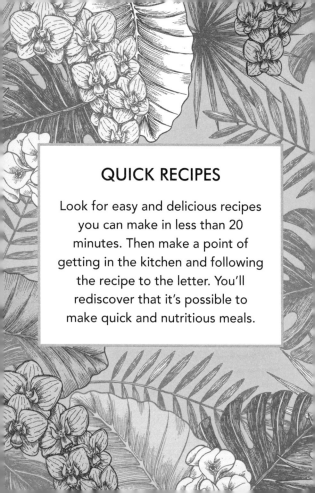

QUICK RECIPES

Look for easy and delicious recipes you can make in less than 20 minutes. Then make a point of getting in the kitchen and following the recipe to the letter. You'll rediscover that it's possible to make quick and nutritious meals.

Posture

Posture can affect your bodily functions more than you realise. These days we spend a lot of time slumped on the sofa or bent over a laptop or phone. Often we hold that position for more than half an hour at a time and sometimes for hours. Stooping or slumping affects our digestion and other bodily functions and can even cause damage to the spinal cord.

A simple solution is to be aware of your position – are you leaning in one direction, or hunching and slumping? Test your posture by tucking in your tailbone and squeeze your shoulder blades together. You can do this sitting, standing or even laying down. Relax into the new position and you'll become very aware of how you were holding your body before. This simple exercise will help you develop a stronger physique overall because your skeleton, muscles and even organs will be properly aligned.

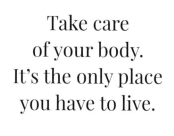

Take care
of your body.
It's the only place
you have to live.

Jim Rohn

Kitchen Experiments

Push the boat out and really experiment with your cooking. Check out paleo, vegan and vegetarian diets and take the tastiest, quickest recipes from each. Grab a notebook and jot down recipe ideas for the week ahead and add ingredients to your shopping list if you need to. This will help you keep on track with buying and eating healthy foods and avoiding unhealthy ready meals.

Be confident in the kitchen and try different ingredients. If a recipe seems really appealing but contains ginger and no one in your household likes ginger, replace it with a different herb or spice. A little thought about the other items in your recipe should steer you in the right direction. Don't be discouraged if you have the odd 'failure' – even the top chefs mess up sometimes!

HYDRATE

Drink plenty of water every day. If the taste doesn't appeal, sometimes a couple of ice cubes will do, or squeeze a little lemon juice in the glass. Avoid adding sugary juices.

I WILL DRINK
AT LEAST
TWO LITRES
OF WATER
EVERY DAY TO
REPLENISH ALL
THE CELLS OF
MY BODY.

Energy Interference

Switch off the gadgets! Avoid having phones and laptops on constant charge, especially in the bedroom. Constant message alerts can, and will, interfere with sleep patterns, as well as break concentration when you are trying to focus on pressing tasks.

Drag your thoughts away from your troubles... by the ears, by the heels, or any other way you can manage it.

Mark Twain

Remedy for worry

Create an atmosphere of calm in your home with the help of an essential oil spritz. Spray it around a room and breathe in the soothing fragrance.

INGREDIENTS:

80–100 drops of essential oils of your choice*
Distilled water
A spray bottle

METHOD:

Simply add water and oil to a spray bottle (the ones you can buy for squirting plants will suffice). Shake the contents well and spray.

*A raft of essential oils can be sourced, each with their own properties. The best for calm are lavender, chamomile, bergamot, frankincense, rose and bergamot.

Yoga

Meditation-based exercise, such as yoga, has been around for many centuries, and science supports its extraordinary benefits. Yoga helps align the body, mind and spirit, and you don't have to be super-bendy or double-jointed to enjoy it! If you don't have the time or inclination for a whole yoga session, pick a posture or two and allow yourself 5 or 10 minutes to strengthen your body. An easy pose is to lie on your back on the floor – make sure there are no draughts – with your legs resting up against a wall. This pose actually helps lower blood pressure as well as generally helping you feel good. Try to do your chosen pose (asana) every day and your body will thank you for it.

If you can find a local yoga class that fits into your lifestyle, join up and meet other like-minded people who want to align their mind, body and spirit as well.

STEP INTO THE FLOW

Make the most of nearby streams, rivers and coastlines and step into them whenever you can. If it's not possible to throw shoes and socks off, simply place your hand in the water and feel the natural flow. This can calm and inspire you at the same time.

Let food be
thy medicine
and medicine
be thy food.

Hippocrates

NATURAL MEDICINE

Natural cough medicine: chop an onion and place in a shallow bowl or saucer with a little brown sugar. Leave overnight, then sip the liquid created by the onion to ease your throat and help soothe your cough.

Natural Remedies

Avoid unnecessary pharmaceuticals if you can – although you should continue taking medicine prescribed by your doctor. It's all too easy to rush into a chemist and buy bottled vitamins and cold remedies. We need certain vitamins every day to keep our bodies healthy but most of these can be found in everyday foods.

Vitamin C can help strengthen your immune system, and prevention is better than cure. We all know that oranges are packed with vitamin C but did you know that parsley – gram for gram – contains more vitamin C than most citrus fruits as well as many other vitamins and minerals, including iron? Eating lots of fruit and veg and incorporating a few cold-preventing herbs in your daily diet will keep your body a lot healthier.

Vitamin C needs to be replenished every day but if we take more than the recommended daily amount the excess will be eliminated by our bodies so it's not possible to cheat and take your weekly amount in just one day!

I AM
NOURISHING
MY BODY WITH
NATURAL
HEALTHY
FOODS
EVERY DAY.

Immune System Boosters

Watercress will help give your immune system a boost and will grow readily in your kitchen, although later you will need some outside space. Buy a bunch of organic watercress to start. Put into a glass of water and refresh daily until roots form, then plant outside. A running water supply is ideal but watercress will grow well in a paddling pool with good drainage. Land cress (a little coarser but just as nutritious) will thrive if planted very close to a running water source.

All leafy green vegetables will give your immune system a boost, and there are usually plenty of varieties available.

Dandelions

All parts of the dandelion 'weed' can be useful. Don't throw them on the compost. The leaves can be eaten, the roots can be roasted and ground into a coffee substitute, the sap inside the stem can be applied to warts and the flowers can be made into a jam!

Remedy for flagging energy

Feeling a bit lacklustre? Pep yourself up with an energising scented shower. Use as much or as little of the oils as you like depending on the strength of scent you prefer.

INGREDIENTS:

Cedar oil
Rosemary oil
Eucalyptus oil
Peppermint oil

METHOD:

Sprinkle droplets of a select combination of essential oils around the base of your shower. As the water heats the cubicle the steam will help the essential oils evaporate and fill the space with a wonderful fragrance. All you need to do is enjoy the power of the water on your skin, and inhale.

If you want an energy boost when you are on the go, simply sprinkle a few drops of the oil of your choice onto a handkerchief or cotton pad ready to sniff when required.

SPIRIT

It's important to be in touch with our spirit even when there is a lot going on around us. It is a lot easier than we think. Information is often just a click away, and we can benefit by researching healthy ways of living for mind, body and spirit. Nourishing your spirit is probably the most fundamental thing you can do to live a joyful life. Many techniques are well-researched and widely practised such as meditation, EFT (emotional freedom technique) and other healing processes that may involve massage, the use of crystals or essential oils. This chapter contains many tips on nurturing your spirit and living the best version of your life.

Emotions

Our emotions are tied into our thoughts and actions. Being aware of how you feel can help you consciously shift your thoughts, and therefore actions, into a positive state which in turn will make you feel better. Often we go through our days with a kind of neutral emotional state until something happens we don't like – which flips us into negative thoughts – or something good happens and we feel happy for a moment or two.

Controlling emotions sounds tricky but can be easy once you master the right techniques. Reactive emotions can lead to stress and all sorts of negative conditions, and reacting instantly when things go wrong could ruin your day. Remember you are worthy of feeling good.

Take a breath and consider whether you'd prefer to feel good or feel bad today. When you choose to feel good, everyone around you will catch the vibe as well!

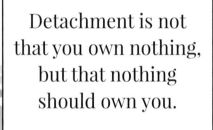

Detachment is not
that you own nothing,
but that nothing
should own you.

Ali bin Abi Talib

COUNT TO TEN

Counting to ten may be an old remedy for diffusing anger but it works! Use the process to bring yourself back to the moment to help you respond rather than react.

APPRECIATE

Think of everything that is positive in your life at this moment. It could be your loved ones or simply a warm home or a job or your new clothes. There is always something you can appreciate.

Gratitude

There is much said and written about the power of gratitude. It is so important to be grateful for everything you have. In today's world, we are encouraged to aspire to acquiring more material possessions all the time. This can create feelings of resentment and frustration when the things we want don't materialise immediately or within a certain period of time, and these negative emotions can even spiral into depression.

Avoid the frustration in the first place by accepting where you are right now and appreciating everything you DO have. You will feel more centred, and the journey to what you want will become clearer and more enjoyable. Enjoying the journey will help you enjoy the destination – a circle of positivity! And when you appreciate those moments along the way, you will find joy around every corner.

Life is simply
a series of moments.
I am enjoying this
moment right now.

Dreams and Goals

Wanting more is a human condition and it's perfectly natural to want more money, love, etc. The more you have the more you can give, and giving really makes you feel good! There are lots of ways to motivate yourself when working towards your goals and dreams. One is to write down what you want to be, do or have, and know the reasons why you want those things.

Simply writing them down won't get to the heart of the matter. Take it one step further and think about why you want those things and really feel the joy and exhilaration you would experience if all those dreams and goals were to come true right now. Give yourself a little quiet time to consider what you'd really like and why. Understanding why you are striving to reach your dreams and goals will help keep you motivated and inspired.

Invest in Yourself

Allow yourself to have desires. You are entitled. You are a creator and can create your own reality. Even if you spend just 5 minutes a day doing something you love, procrastination will take a back seat.

You make a
living by what
you get but you
make a life by
what you give.

Winston Churchill

MOTIVATION

Choose some uplifting and motivational affirmations and create some of your own. For example, if you're trying to increase your income, choose words like 'money flows easily to me now'. Display these affirmations around your home or office.

Shifting Boredom

Sometimes we just don't really know what we want and we get stuck in a rut.

Rather than trying to force a feeling of happiness, make a point of spending some time every day doing something you love and/or feel passionate about. This could be taking another baby step towards the completion of a much-loved project or simply reading a book. Allowing time for yourself every day will help you remember you can find joy and inspiration in any given moment.

I AM THE CREATOR OF MY OWN REALITY.

Meditation

Science has finally confirmed what monks and other spiritual people have known for thousands of years. Meditation is really good for you! It is a practice that needs to be cultivated to work for you but stick with it.

Assign yourself 10 minutes every day to meditate, preferably in the morning before the tasks of the day take over and you get lost in to-do lists. Find a quiet place and sit upright, with your hands in your lap. Touch your thumbs and fingers together – this will help you stay connected – relax your body and focus on a constant sound (this could be an electrical gadget that hums or you could create your own, perhaps with a repetitive 'ohm' sound). If you choose to keep your eyes open, perhaps focus on an open flame. Enjoy the moment and forget about everything else.

MANTRA

Silently chant a mantra that resonates with you to help keep your thoughts from straying. If they do, bring them back gently and repeat your mantra. Try a simple and ancient mantra: 'So Hum' – 'So' on your inhale and 'Hum' on your exhale.

Meditation Moments

Take a few moments during the day at
random times, perhaps while you're
doing the dishes or when you've
finished a task at work and have a
mini meditation moment! Focus solely
on your activity at the time or close
your eyes and relax for a moment.

Remedy for low self-esteem

Rose water is believed to increase feelings of joy and hope and bring a boost to those suffering from low self-esteem. If you could do with a pick-me-up, try relaxing in a warm rose-scented bath and feel your spirits rise. This remedy invites you to make your own bath bomb to enjoy the uplifting scent.

INGREDIENTS:

100 g baking soda
50 g citric acid
25 g rose petals
50 g Epsom salts
1 tsp rose water oil
1 tsp rosehip oil
Red food colouring (optional)
1 tsp water

METHOD:

Place the dry ingredients into a bowl and mix together well. In a separate jug, mix the wet ingredients. Gradually pour the wet ingredients into the dry, stirring constantly. Once all the ingredients are combined pack into a mould of your choice – two small bowls of equal diameter work well if you want to create a ball shape. Allow to dry before adding to a warm bath.

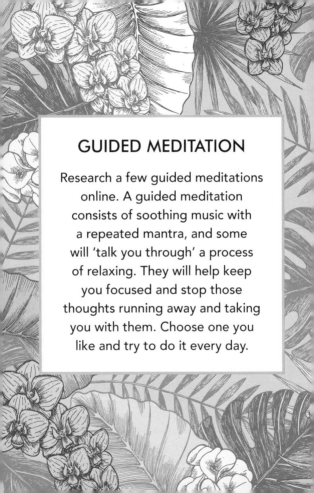

GUIDED MEDITATION

Research a few guided meditations
online. A guided meditation
consists of soothing music with
a repeated mantra, and some
will 'talk you through' a process
of relaxing. They will help keep
you focused and stop those
thoughts running away and taking
you with them. Choose one you
like and try to do it every day.

SERIES OF MOMENTS

Life is a series of moments and although we know this logically, we sometimes forget to apply it to our everyday well-being. Every moment is the only moment we have right now. The following moment is never going to be 'now' again. Remember that this moment can be enjoyable if you choose it to be. When you're ploughing through a chore or a task at work that you'd rather not be doing, remember that this moment will be gone soon and you shouldn't waste it by wishing it away.

By doing this, you put your whole heart and soul into the task at hand and the benefits are twofold: one, you'll probably make a much better job of the task at hand, and two, when you've achieved it, you will feel amazing and fulfilled.

You cannot be
both unhappy
and fully present
in the Now.

Eckhart Tolle

The Ego and You

We all have an ego; it's just a natural trait. We often accuse people of having a big 'ego' or being 'egoic' but it is natural. Our ego controls our mind and develops our personality – which could be problematic if we don't go deeper than the ego from time to time. We need our ego to function in our everyday lives but do you ever have the impression that you are not your thinking mind? That's because you aren't. The ego is like an overlay of who we really are.

Ask yourself a question when you aren't feeling on top of the world, such as 'Is this thought coming from my true self or is it something I have just played along with for a long time and therefore believe it to be part of my character or personality?' Getting in touch with your true self or 'inner being' can throw up all kinds of new ideas and ways forward.

Mirror Work

Love yourself and practise some 'mirror work'. This can feel weird at first but give it a try. Look at yourself in the mirror, keep eye contact and say 'I love you' and use your name. This exercise can dissolve those unworthy feelings that disturb our thoughts. Try it every day.

YOUR HEART'S DESIRE

Consider what you really want.
Not what your mind may be
telling you that you 'should' want,
but drill down to your heart's
desire and run with it all day.

I AM
A WORTHY
BEING.

Serving Others

When you give, your sense of well-being explodes and the feeling can become addictive! Giving doesn't have to mean buying an expensive gift for someone, it could be just picking up the phone and connecting with an old friend to let them know you care.

Giving could be just putting your heart and soul into creating a nutritious healthy meal for the family rather than throwing something in the microwave. It could be buying a sandwich for a homeless person on the street or maybe buying a couple of books in a charity shop. Deciding to do something for someone else every day will boost your spirit and help others at the same time. The ripple effect of a good deed can travel far and wide.

It is
more BLESSED
to GIVE than
to RECEIVE.

Acts 20:35

MAGIC OF NATURE

Take a walk in the forest whenever possible and listen to the sounds and breathe in the scent of the trees and undergrowth. There is a certain magic in trees that we humans tend to ignore for much of the time, but trees provide us with much-needed oxygen and it would be impossible to live without them. Trees grow slowly and can live for thousands of years. Imagine what they could tell us if they could speak our language!

When we appreciate nature we accept the way things are a lot more readily (if a tree has a twisted branch we look at the beauty, we don't judge the tree badly) and it helps us to accept differences in each other as well as being able to enjoy a strong sense of gratitude for nature in all its magnificent glory.

RESPECTING NATURE

Pay your respects to nature. Take a moment to thank the trees for the oxygen you breathe, thank the soil for the fruits and vegetables the earth grows for you every day, and thank the sun for the light and warmth it provides.

THANK YOU
FOR THE
SUNSHINE AND
RAIN AND THE
WONDERS OF
NATURE ALL
AROUND ME.

Dandelion Jam

A traditional French country recipe that insists on 365 flowers but it's worth trying it with about half a tote bag of just the flowers – no leaves or stalks.

INGREDIENTS:

1–2 cooking apples
365 dandelion flowers
1 large or 2 small oranges (or lemons if you
   prefer a sharper taste)
About 750 g of preserving (jam) sugar

METHOD:

Peel and core the apples and put into a large heavy-based saucepan with about three quarters of the flowers. Bring to the boil, reduce heat and simmer for around 10 minutes.

Strain contents of pan through a sieve into a large heat-resistant bowl. Push the flowers and fruit down as much as possible, using the back of a spoon.

Return the strained liquid back to the pan, and add the sugar and juice of lemons or oranges.

Stir over a low heat until the sugar has dissolved.

Remove all the green parts from the rest of the flowers and add to the pan. Bring to the boil.

Boil until the setting point has been reached. To test for setting point, drop a little of the mixture onto a cold saucer. If it forms a light 'skin', setting point has been reached. If not, keep boiling and try again in a few minutes.

Pour carefully into warm prepared sterilised jars. NB: Never pour hot jam into cold jars as the glass will crack.

Seal and label jars and store out of direct light. Jam will keep for about 6 months.

HEALING PLANTS

Dandelions are considered to be a weed but every part of the plant can be used. Many of the plants we walk past every day have healing properties and it's worth learning about them. Google possibilities – but always cross-reference prior to self-medicating.

Get Minimal

Living in a chaotic environment can create chaos in our mind, body and spirit. Where there is clutter, your mind is always making to-do lists, your body has to navigate the untidiness and most importantly, clutter affects your spiritual well-being as it's hard to relax when there is a mountain of stuff piling up around you. Make it a priority to clear the decks. A clear desk is easier to work at. A tidy bedroom is more restful and an organised kitchen helps motivate you into creating healthy meals.

Allocate a weekend or a couple of hours here and there to tidy up. Put things in cupboards where they belong, or hang up clothes that have been piled up on a chair. During this decluttering exercise, think about the items you are tidying and decide if you really need them. Could someone else benefit from a pair of shoes you've never worn, for example? Donate books you've read to the charity shop or pass them on to a friend.

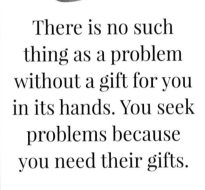

There is no such thing as a problem without a gift for you in its hands. You seek problems because you need their gifts.

Richard Bach

Creativity

Although we are all creative beings, many of us believe we are not 'creative'. This belief often stems from our environment, upbringing and/or media glorification of the 'masters' of the art world. We actually create every day, whether it's filling up the freezer with healthy food or maybe creating our own greetings cards. We are 'natural' creators. Develop your own talents. If you want to learn to play the guitar, go for it. You don't have to aspire to be the next Jimi Hendrix; you just have to enjoy the experience. And you may end up playing at parties and bringing a smile to the faces of your loved ones.

Or you may enjoy knitting or sewing. Find a free pattern online for beginners if you've never done it before and create a unique scarf or cushion cover – you can guarantee no one else will have an identical one!

Bringing
Hobbies to Life

Brainstorm some creative ideas, from scrapbooking to basket-making, from cooking to playing the bongos. See how many you can think of and note which ones felt good to you... follow that one idea and see where it takes you.

I am a spiritual being
having a human
experience.

MEMORIES

Cut out pictures that inspire you from magazines and stick them into a scrapbook, or collect old programmes and theatre tickets that you've collected over the years and keep them in your scrapbook. Alternatively, keep a memory box that you can fill with happy reminders, inspiring images and quotes.

Imagination

We are blessed with an incredible imagination. We tend to discourage ourselves away from imaginative thinking because we think that we should face reality at every moment. But without imagination, nothing would ever be created. Someone somewhere imagined a dress design, a piece of furniture and even the idea that man could create a flying machine. Every creation started in someone's imagination.

Allow your imagination to run wild sometimes. While doing mundane chores think on your dream home or a new business you want to start or that interview you want to go well. Imagination is the birthplace of creative visualisation which can inspire you to take baby steps towards the manifestation you have always wished for. Play with your imagination and have fun.

Remedy to soothe your troubles

Sandalwood is an aromatic wood from which essential oils are derived. It is thought to promote mental clarity and calm when used as a fragrance. This recipe allows you to make your own lotion that you can wear all day long to let the woody scent help you to relax and balance your mood. Simply rub on wrists and ankles to get through a stressful day.

INGREDIENTS:

6 drops sandalwood essential oil
2 drops rose water oil
4 tsp sweet almond oil

METHOD:

Mix the essential oils into the almond oil and store in an airtight jar. Almond oil has been suggested here as it is light and enhances the fragrance of the sandalwood, but a simple vegetable oil can be used in its place.

KINDNESS

The smallest act of kindness can ripple around the world. We all have our own daily chores, problems and issues and it is easy to forget that other people have their own struggles. It's hard to see past our own problems, but putting them on the back burner for a moment or two will give us a different perspective.

An act of kindness is powerful. When you are kind to someone the positive feelings you experience will uplift and inspire you to help someone else. And the person you were kind to will have an upsurge of faith in humanity whereas before they may have doubted the goodness in the world. Start a ripple of kindness today.

INTUITION

Listen to your intuition. When you have a strong gut feeling that something isn't right, trust it and extract yourself from the situation! Alternatively, when it feels good, embrace the idea and let it flow. Meditation can help us to tap into the intuition we all have.

Let the rest
of my life be the
best of my life.

Louise Hay

Smile

As with an act of kindness, a smile is infectious and can travel around the planet if we keep up the momentum. A smile from the heart will make someone's day and they will smile at the next person they meet. If they don't, you will still have spread some love.

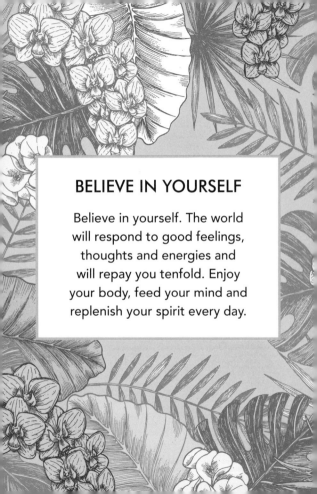

BELIEVE IN YOURSELF

Believe in yourself. The world will respond to good feelings, thoughts and energies and will repay you tenfold. Enjoy your body, feed your mind and replenish your spirit every day.

TODAY
I CHOOSE
FAITH OVER
FEAR.

COMPASSION

Compassion is closely affiliated with kindness. Being mindful that we are all spiritual beings, having a human experience, helps us to understand that none of us is going to get it right every time. Environment influences all of us and depending on our upbringing, financial situation and belief systems, some people, through no fault of their own, find themselves in situations that don't serve them. Be prepared not to take things personally. If someone bumps into you and doesn't stop to apologise, for example, they may be battling with their own demons or perhaps grieving. Take a breath and silently send them a blessing so that they may feel better and you can go on your way without judgemental thoughts or feelings.

CONCLUSION

If you have concerns about your health, please seek professional advice in person from your doctor or local health service. If it feels like nothing is going right at the moment, don't despair. Make a plan and just set one goal for your mind, body or spirit well-being every day and stick to it, however small or insignificant it may feel at the moment. The simple act of improving, baby step by baby step, will build momentum. And before you know it, you will be in the flow and improving every area of your life.

If you're interested in finding out more about our books, find us on Facebook at Summersdale Publishers and follow us on Twitter at @Summersdale.

www.summersdale.com

Image credits